Mandi –
Where would I be without you..?!
thanks for your support and
friendship. You inspire me
daily and I am so grateful
for you–

Clara

FIND YOUR FOCUS

52 Weeks of Clara-ty

CLARA CAPANO

abbott press

Abbott Press books may be ordered through booksellers or by contacting:

Abbott Press
1663 Liberty Drive
Bloomington, IN 47403
www.abbottpress.com
Phone: 1 (866) 697-5310

Because of the dynamic nature of the Internet, any web addresses or links contained in this book may have changed since publication and may no longer be valid. The views expressed in this work are solely those of the author and do not necessarily reflect the views of the publisher, and the publisher hereby disclaims any responsibility for them.

Any people depicted in stock imagery provided by Thinkstock are models, and such images are being used for illustrative purposes only.
Certain stock imagery © Thinkstock.

ISBN: 978-1-4582-2099-8 (sc)
ISBN: 978-1-4582-2100-1 (hc)
ISBN: 978-1-4582-2098-1 (e)

Library of Congress Control Number: 2017905540

Print information available on the last page.

Abbott Press rev. date: 04/28/2017

For Nicholas who brings me love and clarity every day

CONTENTS

Foreword ix

Introduction xi

1   Let Go of the Peanuts 1
2   Wildebeest and Endurance 4
3   The Salesman and the Shoes 6
4   Don't Be Perfect—Be Yourself Perfectly 8
5   Be Responsible 11
6   What's in Your Suitcase? 14
7   Fill Up Your Tank 16
8   Embrace the Wobble 19
9   Jump 21
10 Let It Happen 23
11 The Law of the Garbage Truck 25
12 Struggle a Little 28
13 Break the Leash 30
14 Puzzle Pieces 32
15 Cracks of Gold 34
16 Limitless 36
17 168 Hours 38
18 Ask the Horse 41
19 Light the Logs 43
20 Where Are You Flying To? 45
21 Look in the Dark 47
22 Sweet and Sour 49
23 Crack the Shell 51
24 Commitment Is a Choice 53
25 Fall 56

26 Spider, Spider 58
27 Set Sail 61
28 Off to See the Wizard 64
29 Emergency Brake 66
30 Bamboo Tree 68
31 L Is for Lion 70
32 It Is Possible 72
33 Feed the Right Wolf 74
34 A Lesson from Our Smartphones 76
35 Five Foot Seven 78
36 Open Window 81
37 You Have Enough 83
38 Be Proud 85
39 Welcome to the Dark Side 87
40 The Black Dot 89
41 Welcome Home 92
42 The Bumble Bee 95
43 A Storm Is Coming 97
44 What If? 99
45 Change the Lens 101
46 Move the Boulder 103
47 All of Me 105
48 Let Me Tell You Your Future 107
49 Plant the Tree 109
50 The Orange 111
51 Standing Still 114
52 Grow 116

Closing Thoughts of Clara-ty 119

FOREWORD

Larry Kendall, Author of *Ninja Selling*

Wow! Who is this young woman? I thought the first time I met Clara Capano. *I want her on my team!* Little did I know then that Clara and I would be working together to change people's lives and careers.

Clara Capano is a dynamo—brilliant, passionate, personal, and *focused*! Her system and this book will help you focus so you can be your best. It will literally change your life. I have seen the results with her coaching clients. "Amazing!" "Deep smarts!" "Changed my life!" "Her passion is her calling!" are just a few of the many comments I've received from them.

Focus is the key and also the challenge for most of us. Psychologists report that most Americans are in a continuous state of partial attention. International business coach Robin Sharma puts it this way: "The enemy of Mastery isn't mediocrity. It is distractions. The addiction to distractions ruins many potentially awesome lives." Are you serious about building an awesome life? This book will take you there.

The genius of Clara's system is its simplicity. Everyone can do it. I have used her techniques personally, and she has made a huge difference for me. *Find Your Focus: 52 Weeks of Clara-ty* will make a difference for you as well. Find "Clara-ty" as you clear the clouds of distraction. You will live a happier, healthier, and more purposeful life.

Clara has put her genius into a simple system that will help you get focused so you can be your best in both your business and your life.

INTRODUCTION

Whether you are looking to transform your business or life, *Clara-ty* is the key.

When you're confused or you lack vision or have fear and don't take movement forward, with *Clara-ty* you will

- design and define your vision;
- develop clear and manageable action steps to help you transform; and
- start taking action.

Life isn't always easy, but getting clear should be. It all starts with *Clara-ty*.

People ask why I wrote this book. It's simple: I want to help people. All my life, I've witnessed others (and myself) being stuck. We get in our own way, we sabotage our dreams, and we let our fears hold us back. I want that to change. I want others to feel good about themselves, to get clear on their visions for their life, and to feel empowered to make the change and transformation happen. That's why I wrote this book: to bring you some thoughts and stories that will help to unlock you—to bring you Clara-ty.

How to Use This Book

Find Your Focus is a weekly journal and reflective guide to a better, more fulfilled and productive life. Each week you can read a section and then take time to outline how to put the concepts into play for your business or personal life.

The stories and thoughts are meant to open you up for growth and exploration into becoming the best version of yourself.

Be bold, be brave, and believe in yourself. The *best* of you is yet to come! Finding Clara-ty is the key that will unlock your greatness.

LET GO OF THE PEANUTS

Years ago, a group of scientists observed monkeys in their natural environment. In the study, large glass jars were left out. Each jar had a small opening and was filled with peanuts. The opening was large enough for the monkey to put its hand in but too narrow for it to pull its hand out if it was holding a handful of peanuts. Monkeys love peanuts.

Time after time, the monkeys would come to the jars and reach in for peanuts, and each time, their fists would be too big for them to remove them from the jars. They had a choice to make: drop the peanuts and move on, or stay with their hands stuck in the jars. Time after time, the monkeys would not relinquish the peanuts. Hours would pass, and they would be stuck with their hands in the jars, holding on to the peanuts.

This story reminds me of how we often operate our businesses. We take on clients who have unrealistic goals, are not ready to move forward, are disrespectful, or just plain don't fit into our business model. Instead of dropping them and moving on, we hold on to them like the monkeys to the peanuts. We hold on so tight that we are paralyzed and can't move forward. Why? I think we're afraid that if we let the peanuts (our clients) go, there may not be any more peanuts.

But guess what? There are. The world is full of peanuts. They may be in another jar, in the next village over, or even right under our noses. We just have to know that we have the choice—and the courage—to let go and move on.

So the next time you have a client who is keeping you from moving forward with your business, think about the monkeys. Don't be like the monkeys. Let go of the peanuts.

Journal exercise date: _____/_____/_____

Quote: Be strong enough to let go and patient enough to wait for what you deserve

Takeaway from entry: _____

_____

_____

How does this entry relate to my life (personal or business)? _____

_____

_____

What action steps can I take this week based on this entry? _____

_____

_____

What would make this week great? _____

Notes: _____

_____

_____

2

WILDEBEEST AND ENDURANCE

The plains of Africa are densely populated by wildebeest. More than any other animal, they roam the wild grass for days, searching for water and food. They are not the fastest or the largest animal, yet they are highly successful as a species. Their longevity and success are the result of one key factor: endurance. This animal can last in the heat for long hours and outrun almost any of its predators over long distances.

Endurance keeps our minds going when our bodies want to quit, and it gives us the mental capability and capacity to continue moving forward despite the obstacles, hardships, pain, fatigue, or stress in our paths.

In his book *Surviving the Serengeti*, Stefan Swanepoel illustrates how endurance in business is a key factor to success. Results don't happen overnight. They appear days, weeks, and sometimes months after the initial work begins. We must endure each day with an unwavering dedication to what we do. During times of challenge, we must still show up each day and offer the same value and dedication to all we meet.

Remember that anything worth having, any challenge worth achieving, and any goal worth reaching requires endurance.

They say the strong shall survive. I believe the ones with the endurance to push through and never give up will survive—and more importantly, thrive.

Journal exercise date: _____/_____/_____

Quote: The moment you want to quit is the moment you need to keep pushing.

Takeaway from entry: _____

_____

_____

How does this entry relate to my life (personal or business)? _____

_____

_____

What action steps can I take this week based on this entry? _____

_____

_____

What would make this week great? _____

Notes: _____

_____

_____

THE SALESMAN AND
THE SHOES

Many years ago, two salesmen were sent by a British shoe manufacturer to Africa to investigate and report back on market potential.

The first salesman reported back, "There is no potential here. Nobody wears shoes."

The second salesman reported back, "There is massive potential here. Nobody wears shoes."

This simple short story provides one of the best examples of how a single situation may be viewed in two quite different ways: negatively or positively. Some see a situation's problems and disadvantages instead of its opportunities and benefits.

In today's world, many focus on the negatives: lack of money, stress at home or work, etc. This week I challenge you to take time to see the opportunities rather than the barriers in your business. Now more than ever, people need us. We can bring clarity and value to those around us. We can answer questions, provide support, and help guide people into making good decisions for themselves and their families.

Just like the shoe salesman, look past the barriers, and see the massive opportunities that are in front of you.

Journal exercise date: ____/_____/_____

Quote: Excuses will always be there; opportunities won't.

Takeaway from entry: _____

_____

_____

How does this entry relate to my life (personal or business)? _____

_____

_____

What action steps can I take this week based on this entry? _____

_____

_____

What would make this week great? _____

Notes: _____

_____

_____

DON'T BE PERFECT—BE YOURSELF PERFECTLY

Photos of supermodels—some of the most exquisitely beautiful human beings on the planet—are airbrushed to perfection when they appear in magazines. Despite their chiseled cheekbones, perfect hair, slim figures, and impressive designer outfits, they are often considered too imperfect to appear as is without photographic enhancements.

As a coach and strategist, I work with many who strive for this same perfection in their businesses. I continually hear, "I'll make the calls as soon as I know the script end to end," or "I can't go on a listing until I have my listing presentation perfected." Don't get me wrong—we need to be professionals, and we need to present ourselves as such. But don't hide behind a veil of perfection.

Clients work with you because of who you are: the value you bring and the trust you build with them. They don't want a robot feeding them information or living off a template. They want a real person who can guide them and communicate honestly with them.

In life and in business, there's no such thing as perfection, and no matter how hard you try and how wonderful you are, you will not impress everyone. The good news is that you don't have to. All you need to do is be the trusted adviser they want.

Give yourself a little credit and validation. Be yourself. People will appreciate your sincerity and authenticity.

Journal exercise date: _____/_____/_____

Quote: Be yourself; the world will adjust.

Takeaway from entry: _____

_____

_____

How does this entry relate to my life (personal or business)? _____

_____

_____

What action steps can I take this week based on this entry?_____

_____

_____

What would make this week great?_____

Notes: _____

_____

_____

BE RESPONSIBLE

Coming into the new year, we often perform on a business high. We have goals and plans mapped out, a new energy, and a feeling that a new and promising year lies ahead. But after a couple of weeks, we start to slip. We sleep in a little later; our calls become more sporadic; the needs of the daily schedule become more of a challenge. Where did the energy and zest for the new year go?

Often when we hit the ground running, we face burnout a few weeks into our new plan because it's different, challenging, and outside our comfort zone.

As a coach, I find that people tend to rationalize (very well, I might add) the reasons that keep them from their own success. I hear things like "I've gotten so busy, I don't have time to prospect," "No one wants to buy in the winter; I'll just hit it hard in the spring," or "I don't feel I have the support of my family/spouse/etc."

The thing is, these are all excuses—excuses we have rationalized so well that they sound good and seem like truths in our own minds. What we must remember is that these excuses are not reality; they are, in fact, limiting beliefs—beliefs that keep us from moving further and doing more, beliefs that keep us from our own success.

Here is the reality: *you* are 100 percent responsible for *your* success. It doesn't matter what time of year it is or who does or doesn't support you.

You are the only person who needs to both believe in and be excited about your goals. You alone choose your success.

Is it work? Yes!

Is it hard? Yes!

Is it worth it? Absolutely!

If you're feeling your old feelings and habits creeping back in, step back and ask yourself, "What excuses am I making for myself and my business that are keeping me from success?" Be honest—you deserve it. It is up to you, your commitment, and your enthusiasm. Your success is there.

Journal exercise date: _____/_____/_____

Quote: You are entirely up to you.

Takeaway from entry: _____

_____

_____

How does this entry relate to my life (personal or business)? _____

_____

_____

What action steps can I take this week based on this entry? _____

_____

_____

What would make this week great? _____

Notes: _____

_____

_____

WHAT'S IN YOUR SUITCASE?

One of the things I love to do is travel. At the same time, packing has become a challenge (and sometimes a pain). With airlines charging for excess baggage, it makes all of us take a little more time to plan what we bring with us. Do we really need all that we want to bring with us?

This got me thinking about life and the mental baggage we pack and take with us every day. Do we really need it all?

Every day we take a new journey, and every day we need to repack our mental baggage. How often do we pack things that we don't need: thoughts of the past, fears of clients being lost, illness, family matters, etc.? All of this extra baggage holds us down. It weighs on our minds, our souls, and our hearts. Pack what you do need—love, kindness, enthusiasm, and passion for what you do—and leave behind all the other stuff. You don't need it!

The airlines charge twenty-five dollars, fifty dollars, or more for extra baggage. If we were charged for the extra mental baggage we take with us in life, would we pack differently?

What's in your suitcase today?

Journal exercise date: _____/_____/_____

Quote: If it doesn't matter, get rid of it.

Takeaway from entry: _____

_____

_____

How does this entry relate to my life (personal or business)? _____

_____

_____

What action steps can I take this week based on this entry? _____

_____

_____

What would make this week great? _____

Notes: _____

_____

_____

FILL UP YOUR TANK

In my coaching sessions, one of the comments I hear most is "I'm tired." Trust me; I get it. The market is moving fast, and there isn't much time to get all of the items on our lists done, let alone time to rest. At the same time, taking time to rest and recover is critical to success.

In the book *The Power of Full Engagement*, authors Jim Loehr and Tony Schwartz discuss the concept of managing our energy and not our time. This is quite a different concept for most of us. Many of us believe that time doesn't change and we can't control it. Our response and the energy we put into our time *is* what we can control. They write,

> Balancing stress and recovery is critical in all facets of life. When we expend energy, we draw down our reservoir. When we recover energy, we fill it back up. Too much energy expenditure without recovery leads to burnout and breakdown. Too much recovery without use or sufficient stress leads to atrophy and weakness.

There needs to be balance between the two: equal work and recovery. Here are some tips to help you manage your energy:

1. **Take a time-out each day**. Are you asking, "How and when?" This doesn't have to be a long break—even just twenty to thirty minutes to step away from the phone and computer. You can open a window and breath

in the air, listen to music, call a friend for a fun talk. Just step away and shut your mind down. The world will not fall apart in twenty minutes.

2. **Eat better**. It's true. Eating less fast food and a more balanced diet will give you better energy to face the day. If you're on the run, put a cooler in your car with some fruit, water, and snacks to allow you to grab a quick refuel when you need it.

3. **Work with the "right" people**. You don't need to work with everyone. Take time to make sure you are choosing to work with the right people—those you can help, who want your help, and who value you. Nothing can drain a battery faster than working with the wrong client.

4. **Give yourself a break**. No one is perfect. Neither is life. You can have the best-laid plans for the day, and they can change in an instant. That's okay. Try your best. If you get off track, just breathe and get back on the routine as quickly as you can. At the end of the day, review and reflect on your daily activities. If you did your best, celebrate! It isn't about being perfect; it's about doing the best with what you have.

5. **Ask for help**. I know this is hard for many—me included. This is a busy and crazy world, and we need to support each other. We can't be in two places at once, and it isn't fair to ourselves, our families, or our clients to try to be. If you need help, ask for it. Find a friend, mentor, or guide.

I know all of this seems like common sense, and it's easy to sit here and give advice. So I'll tell you from my heart that I'm working hard to live these tips. It isn't easy, but every day I get up, get focused, and commit to doing my best. I no longer punish myself if I don't get it all done. I just do my best.

Have a good week. Give it your all, and take time to celebrate *you*. You work hard; give yourself some grace.

Journal exercise date: _____/_____/_____

Quote: Balance is not something you find, it is something you Create.

Takeaway from entry: _____

_____

_____

How does this entry relate to my life (personal or business)? _____

_____

_____

What action steps can I take this week based on this entry? _____

_____

_____

What would make this week great? _____

Notes: _____

_____

_____

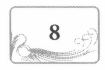

EMBRACE THE WOBBLE

I hadn't been to yoga class for a few days, and my balance was off. Noticing that I was getting frustrated, my instructor told me, "Embrace the wobble." I didn't really know what that meant, but I didn't want to wobble.

She explained it to me after class. When you fight the wobble—or resist the thing that is challenging you—it tends to get worse. When you embrace the wobble rather than fight it, you can more easily move past it. She was right.

In business, we also have a lot of wobbles—things that throw us off balance. The question is, do we focus on those things or just allow them to be so we can move past them? For example, are you focusing on the lower inventory and your clients missing out on properties, or do you accept that and focus on proactive ways to reach out to others to find newer homes that may not be on the market yet?

When you have an appointment, do you wait for the objections around price or commission, or do you focus on the present moment and the questions you're asking so you can best help the person sitting next to you?

There are all sorts of things that can cause us to be off balance in our daily business and what we focus on. If you focus on the wobble, it gets worse. If you just let it be and put your efforts into the present moment, you move more effortlessly. If you focus on the challenge, more obstacles arise. If you focus on the solutions and on being present, opportunity presents itself.

So, for today, embrace the wobble in your business.

Journal exercise date: _____/_____/_____

Quote: What you focus on expands.

Takeaway from entry: _____

_____

_____

How does this entry relate to my life (personal or business)? _____

_____

_____

What action steps can I take this week based on this entry? _____

_____

_____

What would make this week great? _____

Notes: _____

_____

_____

JUMP

If there are six frogs sitting on a lily pad and one decides to jump off, how many are left?

If you answered five, you were incorrect. There would be six. Just because one *decides* to jump off, the action of actually making the leap has not occurred, so the frog is still sitting on the pad

Many of us do the same thing; we think about making a change but fail to follow through with action. I think this is a powerful illustration that we should all take a closer look at. What are you thinking of doing today, this week, this year. And more importantly, what action needs to be done in order for you to complete that action and make the change happen?

Having the desire to do something is one thing; taking action is what defines us and gets us to our goals.

Don't just sit on the lily pad. Take the jump!

Journal exercise date: _____

Quote: Those who don't jump will never fly. (Leena Almashat)

Takeaway from entry: _____

_____

_____

How does this entry relate to my life (personal or business)? _____

_____

_____

What action steps can I take this week based on this entry? _____

_____

_____

What would make this week great? _____

Notes: _____

_____

_____

LET IT HAPPEN

Over the weekend, a thought kept popping up in my life, as it does in the lives of many around me. And the thought was this: *hardship.* Many around me are going through a hardship on some level—maybe in their personal world with a spouse or child, or in their professional world with a challenging client, or with their health.

Hardships are just that—hard. They are challenging, scary, and exhausting, and they often cause us to question all that is around us. But I encourage you to look at hardship in a different way. Rather than seeing it as a negative and something to fight, embrace it and let it guide you.

One of my favorite quotes is "Sometimes the bad things that happen in our lives put us directly on the path to the best things that will ever happen to us."

You see, we need hardship. Hardship allows us to grow, and it helps us to appreciate the good times. Yes, bad things happen and I don't know why. But I do know that something good always comes from it. Maybe today, maybe tomorrow—it will come.

So, if you're struggling with a hardship, take a breath and let it happen. Know that it needs to happen. Don't give up. Have courage. The struggles we face are the things that mold us and create who we are. They make us strong, bring us clarity, and keep us humble.

So for today, don't fight hardship. Believe that something greater is coming to you, because our greatest transformations come out of hardship.

Journal exercise date: _____/_____/_____

Quote: Before something great can happen, it all needs to fall apart.

Takeaway from entry: _____

_____

_____

How does this entry relate to my life (personal or business)? _____

_____

_____

What action steps can I take this week based on this entry? _____

_____

_____

What would make this week great? _____

Notes: _____

_____

_____

THE LAW OF THE GARBAGE TRUCK

One day, a man hopped into a taxi and took off for the airport. Suddenly a car jumped out of a parking space right in front of the taxi. The taxi driver slammed on his brakes, skidded, and missed the other car by just inches. The driver of the other car whipped his head around and started yelling at the taxi driver, who just smiled and waved at him.

So the taxi passenger asked, "Why did you just do that? This guy almost ruined your car and sent us to the hospital!"

The taxi driver said, "The Law of the Garbage Truck." Then he explained, "Many people are like garbage trucks. They run around full of garbage, full of frustration, full of anger, and full of disappointment. As their garbage piles up, they need a place to dump it, and sometimes they dump it on you. Don't take it personally. Just smile, wave, wish them well, and move on."

And don't take on their garbage and spread it to other people at work, at home, or on the streets.

How many times a month, a week, and a day do we allow others to dump their garbage on us? And how often do we hang onto that garbage and let it distract us from the important things in our lives and work?

The bottom line is that successful people don't let garbage trucks take over their day. Each day we have a choice to let others' garbage control us or to block that garbage and live our life.

Stop taking on the garbage! Life is 10 percent what you make it and 90 percent how you take it.

Journal exercise date: ____/____/____

Quote: If you change the way you look at things, the things you look at change. (Dr. Wayne Dyer)

Takeaway from entry: _____

_____

_____

How does this entry relate to my life (personal or business)? _____

_____

_____

What action steps can I take this week based on this entry? _____

_____

_____

What would make this week great? _____

Notes: _____

_____

_____

STRUGGLE A LITTLE

A man found a cocoon of a butterfly. One day, a small opening appeared. He sat and watched the butterfly for several hours as it struggled to squeeze its body through the tiny hole. Then it stopped, as if it couldn't go farther.

So the man decided to help the butterfly. With a pair of scissors, he snipped off the remaining bits of cocoon. The butterfly emerged easily, but it had a swollen body and shriveled wings. The man continued to watch it, expecting that any minute the wings would enlarge enough to support the body. It didn't happened!

In fact, the butterfly spent the rest of its life crawling around. It was never able to fly.

In his kindness and haste, the man didn't understand that the restricting cocoon and the struggle required by the butterfly to get through the opening was a way of forcing the fluid from its body into its wings so it would be ready for flight.

Sometimes struggles are exactly what we need. Going through life with no obstacles would cripple us. Without them, we won't be as strong as we could have been. And we will never fly.

So have a nice day, and don't be afraid to struggle a little.

Journal exercise date: _____/_____/_____

Quote: Where there is no struggle, there is no strength.

Takeaway from entry: _____

_____

_____

How does this entry relate to my life (personal or business)? _____

_____

_____

What action steps can I take this week based on this entry? _____

_____

_____

What would make this week great? _____

Notes: _____

_____

_____

BREAK THE LEASH

For years, an owner kept his dog on a leash that was twenty feet long. The dog could run and play and chase squirrels until they went past the twenty-foot mark. After a few years, the owner felt bad and decided to let the dog off the leash. As the dog sat in the yard with freedom to run, it remained confined to the twenty-foot boundary it had lived in for years. In the dog's mind, it could go only that far and no farther. So it stayed confined to the limit it had in its mind.

Like the dog, we often set limits on how far we can go. We don't see that we can be great and accomplish things others have only dreamed of. We have become chained and confined like the dog—never knowing the success and the joy of all we can create.

What are your limits? Are you holding yourself back? Have you chained yourself up, not allowing yourself to run free? Take a moment to identify your limits and what holds you back. Is it fears? Did someone tell you that you couldn't do something? Or maybe you have a dream that seems unattainable.

Then use today to break from your chains. Allow yourself to run free and break through the limits you or others have set. You can have it all!

Journal exercise date: _____/_____/_____

Quote: Limits, like fears, are often just an illusion. (Michael Jordan)

Takeaway from entry: _____

_____

_____

How does this entry relate to my life (personal or business)? _____

_____

_____

What action steps can I take this week based on this entry? _____

_____

_____

What would make this week great? _____

Notes: _____

_____

_____

PUZZLE PIECES

As a kid, I spent a lot of time working on puzzles with my sister. I always dreaded the beginning: looking at all the pieces and feeling overwhelmed about where to start. When you put a large puzzle together, it's difficult at first to decipher where certain pieces will go.

I always started with the borders; they're easy. The oddly shaped pieces in the middle didn't seem to have a place when there were no outlines to fit them into. But after a time, when more of them fit together, it all began to make sense. And at the end, every piece fit in its own perfect space.

Life is often like this. When you begin a new project, start a new job, etc., the beginning can be hard. You don't always know how you fit in or if the new venture will pay off. But as you start to place the pieces, the image starts to become clear. First a small corner, then the backdrop—and eventually the puzzle is complete.

Too many of us stop midway through the process. We get bored, frustrated, annoyed, or distracted. We tell ourselves it takes too long to finish or that it's too hard. And we walk away, leaving our goals, dreams, and actions unfinished.

Make the commitment to yourself not to walk away. Stay and finish the puzzle. In time, the pieces will come together and fit into a beautiful finished picture.

Journal exercise date: _____/_____/_____

Quote: Motivation gets you started; commitment keeps you going.

Takeaway from entry: _____

_____

_____

How does this entry relate to my life (personal or business)? _____

_____

_____

What action steps can I take this week based on this entry? _____

_____

_____

What would make this week great? _____

Notes: _____

_____

_____

CRACKS OF GOLD

In Japan, when something breaks, they glorify the damage by filling the cracks with gold. They believe that when something has been broken, it has history and therefore becomes more beautiful.

How many of us have suffered a setback or felt broken or damaged? And how many times during those moments have we beaten ourselves up and had difficulty moving forward?

We all have setbacks. There are times when our days are hard. We feel defeated and wonder if we can—or even want to—go on. But what if, instead of focusing on the failure or being broken, we looked at the setback as a thing of beauty, a chance to refocus and grow? What if we choose not to beat ourselves up, but rather to move forward, learning from our actions and becoming stronger?

This week, fill your cracks with gold. See the beauty in your setbacks, and become even more beautiful and strong.

Journal exercise date: _____/_____/_____

Quote: The setback is the comeback for your future.

Takeaway from entry: _____

_____

_____

How does this entry relate to my life (personal or business)? _____

_____

_____

What action steps can I take this week based on this entry? _____

_____

_____

What would make this week great? _____

Notes: _____

_____

_____

LIMITLESS

A couple of years ago, a movie called *Limitless* hit the theaters. The main character was offered a pill that would make him "limitless," and it gave him the ability to do anything he desired: learn languages, succeed in business, get fit. And he accomplished all of those things.

If you were offered this pill, would you take it? Would you choose to be limitless?

After thinking about this question, I realized that we are all *already* limitless. Anything we want to do, anything we want to have, we can. If I want to learn a language, I can. If I want to get more in shape and in better health, I can. If I want to be more successful, I can.

There is no pill for this, but the ability to be limitless is already there. It's in the daily choices you make; it's in the people you associate with; it's in your inner desire to be your best. It will take work and dedication and passion, and you will have to do this work every day.

Sometimes your greatest limit is you. Today make the choice to be limitless.

Journal exercise date: _____/_____/_____

Quote: I *am* limitless.

Takeaway from entry: _____

_____

_____

How does this entry relate to my life (personal or business)? _____

_____

_____

What action steps can I take this week based on this entry? _____

_____

_____

What would make this week great? _____

_____

Notes: _____

_____

_____

168 HOURS

I'm reading a book called _168 Hours,_ and _wow,_ is it eye opening! It discusses that in any given week, we all have roughly 168 hours to live our life. It really got me thinking. How am I _really_ spending my time?

I have always considered myself to be somewhat of a taskmaster, but I felt like time was slipping away and moving too fast. I needed a reset, a way to help me refocus and not look for more hours in the day. I also needed to be honest with myself about how I was spending my 168 hours.

Time is a resource—and once it's gone, it's gone. You can't get it back. Ever. So let's look at how we can use our 168 hours:

- Work: 40 hours
- Time with family: 35 (5 hours a day for morning routine, dinner, etc.)
- Exercise: 5 (1 hour/5 days a week)
- Community: 2 (church, volunteer, etc.)
- Personal/ leisure time (yes, you are due some): 10
- Sleep: 56 (8/day)

That totals 148 hours, leaving twenty hours—almost a whole day!

Seeing this was pretty powerful for me. It was both enlightening and a little depressing. I had to be honest with myself about how I was wasting that extra day—or rather, not using it wisely.

So I ask you to look at your 168 hours. Are you using them wisely? Are you spending your time with the right people and in areas that will enrich your life and impact others? Are you taking time to reflect and reenergize yourself?

You see, there really is enough time for it all. We just have to make the decision to make it so. I'm not saying it will be easy or it will not take some thought and discipline. But if you want to "find" more time in your day, take a look at how you're using your hours—I mean, really using your hours.

So I ask you again, how are you spending your 168 hours this week?

Journal exercise date: _____/_____/_____

Quote: Lost time is never again found. (Benjamin Franklin)

Takeaway from entry: _____

_____

_____

How does this entry relate to my life (personal or business)? _____

_____

_____

What action steps can I take this week based on this entry? _____

_____

_____

What would make this week great? _____

Notes: _____

_____

_____

ASK THE HORSE

A man was riding a horse, which was galloping very quickly. An onlooker he passed shouted, "Where are you going in such a hurry?"

The rider replied, "I don't know. Ask the horse!"

This story reflects most people's lives. They are riding the horse fast and have no real idea where they're headed. They haven't stopped to identify where they want to go or even the habits they need to get there. They just jump on and let someone else or something else lead them.

It's time to take the reins and take control of your life! No more living on autopilot. It's time to make plans, create good habits (or get back to those habits if you've strayed), and go in the direction *you* want to go.

For this week, live with purpose. Take time to reassess your goals and habits, and then take the action to follow through. Don't give your direction to someone else.

Journal exercise date: _____/_____/_____

Quote: When you have control over your thoughts, you have control over your life.

Takeaway from entry: _____

_____

_____

How does this entry relate to my life (personal or business)? _____

_____

_____

What action steps can I take this week based on this entry? _____

_____

_____

What would make this week great? _____

Notes: _____

_____

_____

LIGHT THE LOGS

There was a man sitting in his living room in the dark. When his wife came in and asked why he was sitting in the dark, his response was that he thought there would be light from the fireplace. Her response: "Well, there will be, but first you need to light it."

This isn't only a funny story; it also relates to our business and life. We can't wait around for things to happen; we need to go and make it happen. We have to light our own fireplace. We have to get up and make the calls, write the notes, and make the appointments happen.

I know at times we feel we're doing all these things, yet nothing is happening. This is where I ask you to have patience. Sometimes change and getting the results we want takes time, and there may be obstacles. When lighting a fireplace, sometimes there's a draft or the logs are damp, so it takes time for the fire to ignite. But have patience and faith, because when the fire does catch hold, it will burn strong and bright.

For this week, ask what you are going to do to light the fireplace?

Journal exercise date: _____/_____/_____

Quote: Patience is bitter, but its fruit is sweet. (Aristotle)

Takeaway from entry: _____

_____

_____

How does this entry relate to my life (personal or business)? _____

_____

_____

What action steps can I take this week based on this entry? _____

_____

_____

What would make this week great? _____

Notes: _____

_____

_____

WHERE ARE YOU FLYING TO?

Did you know that airplanes are off course 90 percent of the time? Ninety percent! And you know what else? They still arrive at their destination. So how do they do this? The pilots continually monitor the desired path and make corrections along the way. They may have to adjust for weather or other air traffic. They know that even if they go off course a little, all they have to do is correct and get back on course.

Do you ever get pulled off your flight path? I bet you do. I know I do, and it's probably pretty close to the same 90 percent that pilots do.

You see, that's life. We all get pulled off track due to family, work, health, etc. However, we can have a plan. True professionals don't get derailed by the fact they got pulled off track; rather, they autocorrect along the way. They make choices that are smart and allow them flexibility, and they still arrive at the desired destination.

So for this week, have a plan! Don't focus on all that can happen to pull you off your path. Just do your best. Autocorrect along the way, and stay connected with the destination. It isn't about being 100 percent on track. It's about doing your best and having a clear path to your destination.

Happy flying!

Journal exercise date: _____/_____/_____

Quote: If plan A didn't work, there are twenty-five more letters in the alphabet. Stay cool.

Takeaway from entry: _____

_____

_____

How does this entry relate to my life (personal or business)? _____

_____

_____

What action steps can I take this week based on this entry? _____

_____

_____

What would make this week great? _____

Notes: _____

_____

_____

LOOK IN THE DARK

There was a man on top of a hill. He was on his knees, looking through the tall grass. A friend approached him and asked, "My friend, what are you looking for?"

The man replied, "My keys."

Wanting to help, his friend inquired, "Well, where is the last place you remember seeing them?"

The man stopped and looked over his shoulder to the forest. It was dark and full of tall trees. "I believe the last place was over there, in the forest."

His friend asked with concern, "Then why, my friend, are you looking here on the hill?"

Embarrassed, the man responded, "Because this is where the light is."

Often we look for answers where there's light. We think the light will bring us clarity, because in the light we're safe. However, often all our answers are hidden in the dark, and we're afraid to look there. We're afraid because it's uncertain and unfamiliar. But it is where the answers are found, more often than not.

This week, don't be afraid to look in the dark. You may just find what you're looking for.

Journal exercise date: _____/_____/_____

Quote: I am my problem, but I am also my solution.

Takeaway from entry: _____

_____

_____

How does this entry relate to my life (personal or business)? _____

_____

_____

What action steps can I take this week based on this entry? _____

_____

_____

What would make this week great? _____

Notes: _____

_____

_____

SWEET AND SOUR

Last week I had a missed opportunity with a client. It threw me for a loop, and I allowed it to derail my focus and lead me into the rabbit hole of questions: What did I do wrong? What signs did I miss? What could I have done better?

A friend he told me, "You can't have the sweet without the sour." I think what he was trying to tell me was that the wins in life are made that much better by the fact they are balanced by the hard times. If it weren't for the challenges, how would we be able to recognize the good times? He was right.

In all aspects of our lives—personal and professional—we have both the sweet and the sour, the wins and the losses, the ups and the downs. That's just part of life.

So, this week, if you have a challenge, embrace it and be grateful for it. That challenge will make the next win even more glorious.

Journal exercise date: _____/_____/_____

Quote: If it doesn't challenge you, it won't change you.

Takeaway from entry: _____

_____

_____

How does this entry relate to my life (personal or business)? _____

_____

_____

What action steps can I take this week based on this entry? _____

_____

_____

What would make this week great? _____

Notes: _____

_____

_____

CRACK THE SHELL

For a seed to complete its full expression, it must become completely undone. It must break through the shell and leave itself exposed. This is where growth and its true potential are achieved.

We too crack out of our shells to reach our greatness. We have to be brave and face our fears, believe in our own self, and let go of the things that are no longer serving us. Too many times we stay inside the shell of our potential. We feel we are safe and protected inside. But actually we aren't allowing ourselves to grow, to transform, and to become the best version of ourselves.

To become who we are destined to be, we must be brave and crack the shell. We must fully expose ourselves. Yes, it can be scary and hard, but when you break through, you begin to see all the greatness and possibilities of the world and the true gifts you can bring.

This week, break through. Don't hold back. Be great! Allow growth to happen.

Journal exercise date: _____/_____/_____

Quote: A comfort zone is a beautiful place, but nothing ever grows there.

Takeaway from entry: _____

_____

_____

How does this entry relate to my life (personal or business)? _____

_____

_____

What action steps can I take this week based on this entry? _____

_____

_____

What would make this week great? _____

Notes: _____

_____

_____

COMMITMENT IS A CHOICE

Commitment isn't something you wake up with; it's something you choose.

The last few days, I've been hearing a lot about life-altering events that make people *finally* change: death, divorce, loss of a job, jail, bankruptcy, hitting rock bottom. The pain becomes so strong, there's no other option but to change.

It seems that before we commit to something, we tend to justify why we can't commit 100 percent. We use lack of time, lack of money, responsibilities, etc. How can we ever fully commit if before we even start we have already given ourselves several ways out?

We all stumble and make mistakes, but let's not settle for just giving part of ourselves. Give it all! You are worth more!

What is your *why*? What gets you excited to wake up each morning and fills your soul with joy?

I commit today that my *why* is strong enough that I don't need a life-altering event. My *why* is this: I want balance and excellence in finances, life, health, and love for my family and me. I want the freedom to put my time and money into the people I love and care about. I want to add joy, love, and peace to those around me. I want to help others in whatever way they need. I want to make a difference in the world.

Why are you waiting for your happiness, your success, your dreams? Start today, and give today all you've got. What is your *why*, and is it strong enough to push you to give 100 percent every day?

Remember, someday isn't a day of the week. Make today count!

Journal exercise date: _____/_____/_____

Quote: Commitment means staying loyal to what you said you would do long after the mood you said it in has left you.

Takeaway from entry: _____

_____

_____

How does this entry relate to my life (personal or business)? _____

_____

_____

What action steps can I take this week based on this entry? _____

_____

_____

What would make this week great? _____

Notes: _____

_____

_____

FALL

I was at a skate park with my son the other day, and there was another child who just blew me away. He was about four and was decked out with his skateboard in tow. He went to make a jump and—well, didn't land it. He hit the ground so hard that all of the parents around stopped to see if we needed to rush over and help him.

To our surprise, he not only got up, he got up and with the biggest smile looked at his dad and yelled, "Did you see that?! I almost got it that time." And off he went to try again.

He tried that same jump several times but never landed it—and he also never gave up. Each time he went back with the same smile and same determination. After each fall, he got up.

How many times did you fall last week, last month, this year? And did you get back up with enthusiasm and determination to try again, or did you allow the fall to keep you down?

We all fall down. Sometimes it's easy to shake it off, and other times the pain lingers. But we have to keep getting up.

Falling down keeps us strong. It keeps us fighting for what we want, and it pushes us to grow. If we never fall, we never have a chance to improve. Falling is a part of life. Living is about getting up!

This week, don't focus on the fall. Just focus on getting back up.

Journal exercise date: _____/_____/_____

Quote: Never give up. Great things take time.

Takeaway from entry: _____

_____

_____

How does this entry relate to my life (personal or business)? _____

_____

_____

What action steps can I take this week based on this entry? _____

_____

_____

What would make this week great? _____

_____

Notes: _____

_____

_____

26

SPIDER, SPIDER

To self-disclose a bit, I have a strong dislike for spiders. My son, however, finds them fascinating, so I've had to learn to accept them into my world. Outside our house we have a garden spider that has built a large web. Every morning she's there in her web to greet the day.

One night we had a bad rainstorm, and in the morning the web was gone. Not thinking much of it, I moved on with my day. The next morning, to my surprise, the spider was back with a new web of the same size, as if nothing had damaged the first one.

A couple days later—another rainstorm and another damaged web. But alas, the next morning back it was. This happened several more times. The rain came, and the spider kept building her web. I have to say that impressed me. Here's this tiny creature whose home and effort was destroyed not once, not twice, but several times. Yet back she came and rebuilt each time.

She would stay up all through the night so that it was there the next day in full force. That's commitment! She knew she needed that web to survive, and even though she could have moved it to a more protected place, she stayed and rebuilt.

How many times have you had your world damaged—lost a big client, failed at a presentation, lost an opportunity? Did you come back and stay committed?

Every day the rain will come in some form, and it will threaten to destroy your world. But like the spider, you can't run away. You must come back and be strong enough to rebuild. Day after day, storm after storm, you must come back and face the storms. With each one, you will become stronger and more resilient. The rain will eventually pass, and the sun will come out, and there you'll be.

Don't let the storm beat you. Be like my little spider friend; come back each day and rebuild your world. You are tougher than the rain.

Journal exercise date: _____/_____/_____

Quote: Don't be afraid to start over. It's a chance to rebuild what you really want.

Takeaway from entry: _____

_____

_____

How does this entry relate to my life (personal or business)? _____

_____

_____

What action steps can I take this week based on this entry? _____

_____

_____

What would make this week great? _____

Notes: _____

_____

_____

27

SET SAIL

According to legend, Spanish conquistador Hernán Cortés issued an interesting order to his men as they began their conquest of the Aztec empire in 1519. As they landed on enemy soil, prepared to fight, he ordered the men to burn the ships they'd used to sail across the sea. That's right—he ordered them to burn their own ships!

Legend has it that, as they burned, he told them something like this: "You see the boats going up in smoke. That means we cannot leave these shores alive unless we win! We now have no choice—we win or we perish."

You see, with no escape route, the soldiers realized they must give it their all and raise their standards. There was no alternative for them. With that, they succeeded in their mission and were victorious.

How many of us have boats waiting in the harbor? How many times have we retreated to the safety of the harbor when things got tough? The reality is that we all do this from time to time. But what if we burned those boats? What if we had no other option but to move forward, because there was no safety net, no escape, no excuses waiting to keep us safe and to allow us to retreat?

What are your boats? Is there anything you're keeping in the harbor that allows you to retreat to safety? If so, burn it! Getting rid of that escape will be scary, *and* it will also free you. It will allow you to dig deep and find your courage, your strength, and your determination to fight.

This week, stand tall and raise your standard. Burn your ships, and see how far you can sail on your own.

Journal exercise date: _____/_____/_____

Quote: Don't look back; you aren't going that way.

Takeaway from entry: _____

_____

_____

How does this entry relate to my life (personal or business)? _____

_____

_____

What action steps can I take this week based on this entry? _____

_____

_____

What would make this week great? _____

Notes: _____

_____

_____

28

OFF TO SEE THE WIZARD

As a kid, I watched the movie *The Wizard of Oz* more than a hundred times. I loved how Dorothy found her way home and that she did it with the help of her three friends, or guides: the Scarecrow (the brain), the Tin Man (the heart) and the Lion (courage). Without these three by her side, she would have been alone and lost.

Don't we all have and need these three friends in our daily lives:

1. Our brain helps us make good decisions.
2. Our heart reminds us of our passion.
3. Our courage pushes us through the hard times and challenges.

Each week and every day, we follow our own path. Sometimes it's filled with joy, and other times flying monkeys scare us and take us off course. Either way, all we need to do is look to our friends, and we will be able to find our way home.

This week, what lies ahead for you? Are you using your brain to plan your week so you can make good decisions? Are you using your heart so you can stay energized and passionate about what to do and who you can serve? And do you have the courage to fight off anything that may cause you to stumble?

Like Dorothy, you aren't alone; you have all you need with you. You don't need the wizard of Oz or ruby slippers (although a good pair of shoes is always advised). To find your way, just connect with your three friends, and you will always be okay.

Journal exercise date: _____/_____/_____

Quote: Trust the process; your time is coming. Do the work, and the results will handle themselves. (Tony Gaskins)

Takeaway from entry: _____

_____

_____

How does this entry relate to my life (personal or business)? _____

_____

_____

What action steps can I take this week based on this entry? _____

_____

_____

What would make this week great? _____

Notes: _____

_____

_____

EMERGENCY BRAKE

Have you ever driven with the emergency brake on? If so, your car likely struggled to move forward and couldn't perform the way it was intended. It was held back.

Many of us drive our business every day the same way: we have our own internal emergency brake. It shows up in the form of *but*.

I would love to do that, but I need more money.

I would love to have success, but I'm new at this.

I want to have more time for activities, but I'm too busy.

We *but* ourselves into a halted state every day. That emergency brake keeps us from the life and success we really want. We think the brake is keeping us safe from danger—from rolling away out of control. But the reality is that it stops us and makes it harder for us to move forward to the good things and the accomplishments we can—and should—attain.

The good news is this: you *can* release the brake. Yup, that's right. You can let it go. And once you do, you will be able to move forward effortlessly.

This week, let go of the brake. Drive free. Enjoy the ride.

Journal exercise date: _____/_____/_____

Quote: Some of us think holding on makes us strong, but it really is in letting go. (Herman Hess)

Takeaway from entry: _____

_____

_____

How does this entry relate to my life (personal or business)? _____

_____

_____

What action steps can I take this week based on this entry? _____

_____

_____

What would make this week great? _____

Notes: _____

_____

_____

BAMBOO TREE

The Chinese bamboo tree takes five years to grow. For the first year, you water it, feed it, and nothing happens. For the second year, again you feed, water, and nurture it—and nothing happens. The third and fourth year? Same thing. In year five, however, the roots finally take hold, and the tree grows three feet in one day. So the question many ask is, did it take five years or one day for the tree to grow?

I believe the tree started to grow five years ago. Without the nurturing, it would not have the energy and power to finally sprout and grow to its true ability.

A business is much like this. We show up daily and feed it yet may not see results. Only after consistent feeding and nurturing does the magic happens, and it takes root and grows strong. As we do with the little bamboo tree, we can't give up or stop feeding our business, because we risk the roots not taking hold.

It's hard to show up every day and see little results. We question if it will ever work, and we wonder if we are doing something wrong. But if you believe in your process, and you show up with passion daily and do the right things, the roots will be there. You may not see them, but with every day, your tree is growing stronger and eventually will take hold in the ground and grow mighty and strong.

Journal exercise date: _____/_____/_____

Quote: Brilliant results don't just show up by chance. The finest things in life take patience, focus, and sacrifice. (Robin Sharma)

Takeaway from entry: _____

_____

_____

How does this entry relate to my life (personal or business)? _____

_____

_____

What action steps can I take this week based on this entry? _____

_____

_____

What would make this week great? _____

Notes: _____

_____

_____

L IS FOR LION

Even the king of the jungle needs a plan. The majestic lion isn't guaranteed a meal—eating takes strategy. If the lion (or lioness) doesn't approach the situation with a strategy and execute the plan correctly, it will go hungry. Success (a.k.a. dinner) isn't guaranteed.

The same is true for us and the goals we want to accomplish: we must have a strategy. So I ask, do you have a plan, a strategy to be successful? Even as you approach this week, have you identified what it will take to hit your targets?

My challenge for you this week is to have a clearly written plan, to review your plan, and to show up daily with a strategy. This is your life; don't shortchange yourself and what you can accomplish by not showing up prepared and ready to fight for what you want.

Be a lion this week. Be ready to take on the week with fight. Know what you need to do first—then go do it!

Journal exercise date: _____/_____/_____

Quote: Every battle is won before it starts. (Sun Tzu)

Takeaway from entry: _____

_____

_____

How does this entry relate to my life (personal or business)? _____

_____

_____

What action steps can I take this week based on this entry? _____

_____

_____

What would make this week great? _____

_____

Notes: _____

_____

_____

IT IS POSSIBLE

This weekend, I had the pleasure of going to a Cirque du Solei performance. It was *amazing*. As I sat on the edge of my seat, eyes glued to the stage, watching the performers, my internal voice kept saying, "How do they do that? That's impossible!" With each new performance, they amazed me with moves and tricks that just did not seem possible.

Then it dawned on me: the performers were experts at making the impossible possible.

Take a moment to think about you and your world. What seems impossible to you? Is it taking on a new challenge, working with a new client, or changing how you normally run your business? No matter what it is, don't think of it as impossible, because chances are you can make it possible.

This week, make your impossible feat possible!

Journal exercise date: _____/_____/_____

Quote: Nothing is impossible. The word itself says "I'm possible." (Audrey Hepburn)

Takeaway from entry: _____

_____

_____

How does this entry relate to my life (personal or business)? _____

_____

_____

What action steps can I take this week based on this entry? _____

_____

_____

What would make this week great? _____

Notes: _____

_____

_____

33

FEED THE RIGHT WOLF

This week I learned a new fable. You have two wolves: one can live only in the light and the other only in the dark. Which one will survive? The answer: whichever one you feed.

Daily we face decisions that lead us into the light or into the dark. Here are some examples:

- Do I choose to get up and work out or hit the snooze button?
- Do I work with this client or gracefully decline, knowing he doesn't trust in me or my process.
- Will I believe in myself?

You see, our success in life greatly depends on the decisions we make and the wolf we choose to feed. There is light and dark in all things. That will never change, but how you decide which to focus on can change.

This week, look at the decisions you make. Are they leading you into your light or keeping you lost in the dark?

Make sure you're feeding the right wolf for you and your goals.

Journal exercise date: _____/_____/_____

Quote: Your life is a result of the choices you've made.

Takeaway from entry: _____

_____

_____

How does this entry relate to my life (personal or business)? _____

_____

_____

What action steps can I take this week based on this entry? _____

_____

_____

What would make this week great? _____

Notes: _____

_____

_____

A LESSON FROM OUR SMARTPHONES

Many of us have a smartphone, and on that phone we have applications (apps). How many times a week do you get a request to update an app on your phone? The reason is that the creators of the app are continually improving it. That's fantastic!

But do you know what they didn't do? They didn't wait until the app was perfect before letting it go live.

That's right. When they set it free to the public, it wasn't perfect. They knew that in that moment, the app was as perfect as it could be and that there would be additions and improvements along the way—*and that was okay*. They would just update as they improved.

How many times have you waited to do something, say something, or launch something because it wasn't perfect? Often we sell ourselves into a false security by thinking we're protecting ourselves by waiting, but here is the reality: no matter how perfect something is, if it's unknown to others, it's useless.

So this week, don't wait for perfection. Give your best. Promote your tools and ideas. Go out and let the world see you.

It doesn't have to be perfect; it just has to be your best.

Journal exercise date: _____/_____/_____

Quote: You were born to be real, not perfect.

Takeaway from entry: _____

_____

_____

How does this entry relate to my life (personal or business)? _____

_____

_____

What action steps can I take this week based on this entry? _____

_____

_____

What would make this week great? _____

Notes: _____

_____

_____

35

FIVE FOOT SEVEN

I am vertically challenged. Yep, I'm short. Five feet even—to be exact. In fact, my whole family is short—anyone five eight would be considered a giant. My father, however, always said to me, "Five seven, Clara," as I walked by him. It wasn't because I was slouching or because he was trying to place some Italian mojo on me to grow taller than the other family members. It was to remind me to always walk with my head high and know that, regardless of physical size, I can own whatever situation I'm in. This phrase has always stuck with me.

To get through life, you have to stand tall. People try (sometimes successfully) to knock or pull you down, and you must not only rise back up, but continue to stand tall. So "five seven" has lots of meanings:

- Have belief in yourself.
- Have conviction and passion for what you are doing.
- Know you are loved.
- Be bold.
- Take charge.
- Live with grace in all you do.
- Be kind.
- Be and give your absolute best every day.

This week, I challenge you to walk tall and take charge. Know what you need to accomplish, and believe in yourself in all you do. I'll never be tall, but I can always hold my head high and accomplish great things. And so can you!

Thanks, Dad, for this valuable lesson.

Journal exercise date: _____/_____/_____

Quote: I faced it all. I stood tall. I did it my way. (Frank Sinatra)

Takeaway from entry: _____

_____

_____

How does this entry relate to my life (personal or business)? _____

_____

_____

What action steps can I take this week based on this entry? _____

_____

_____

What would make this week great? _____

Notes: _____

_____

_____

OPEN WINDOW

What would you do if you arrived home and realized you didn't have your house key? Would you just stand outside? No, you would walk around your house and look for a way in. You would look for an open window, test the garage door, or check the back door. You would know that the front door is not the only way into the house; you would know that there could be another alternative.

However, in business and life, when we show up without our key, we often pack it up and leave. We think there is only one way to do something, and we don't have the vision to look at alternate ways around the problem. But the reality is, there is always another option, another way to find a solution.

This week, what challenges are you facing? Are you just standing in front of your locked door? Discover another approach, and look for new resources and people who can help you. Don't be afraid to look for another way in.

Journal exercise date: _____/_____/_____

Quote: The more obstacles I overcome, the stronger I become. (Grace Alvarez)

Takeaway from entry: _____

_____

_____

How does this entry relate to my life (personal or business)? _____

_____

_____

What action steps can I take this week based on this entry? _____

_____

_____

What would make this week great? _____

Notes: _____

_____

_____

YOU HAVE ENOUGH

"A very large quantity of something." That is how a dictionary defines *abundance*. Life coach Chris Lee has a different definition: abundance is a state of conscious gratefulness. Basically, abundance is about gratitude. It's focusing on all the things we have and being grateful for the life and opportunities we have each day.

- Being grateful that we woke up in a warm bed
- Being grateful that we have food and clean water
- Being grateful that we have our health and body to be able to work out
- Being grateful that we have friends, client, mentors around us daily

Being grateful for it all, because even though it isn't always perfect, many would die to have the gifts that we have.

In reality, we all have enough. It's just a matter of focusing on what we have instead of on what we're missing.

This week, live in abundance. Pay attention to the gifts, opportunities, joy, love, and all that you do have. My guess is that as you do this, you'll know you have some amazing things.

Journal exercise date: _____/_____/_____

Quote: When you are grateful, abundance appears and fear disappears. (Tony Robbins)

Takeaway from entry: _____

_____

_____

How does this entry relate to my life (personal or business)? _____

_____

_____

What action steps can I take this week based on this entry? _____

_____

_____

What would make this week great? _____

Notes: _____

_____

_____

BE PROUD

Pride is "a feeling or deep pleasure or satisfaction derived from one's own achievements, the achievements of those with whom one is closely associated, or from qualities or possessions that are widely admired." Many of us have pride and are comfortable stating our pride in our families, work, and other accomplishments. However, you might struggle with being proud of yourself—the person you are.

Somewhere, as we grew up, we were taught that it's selfish and inappropriate to talk about being proud of ourselves. Doing it means we're vain or conceited?

But why shouldn't we be proud of ourselves? We work hard and should accept our successes. We should live in our light and not diminish it.

This week, be proud! Be proud of who you are and all you have accomplished and will accomplish.

Journal exercise date: _____/_____/_____

Quote: Don't wait until you reach your goal to be proud of yourself. Be proud of every step you take. (Karen Salmansohn)

Takeaway from entry: _____

_____

_____

How does this entry relate to my life (personal or business)? _____

_____

_____

What action steps can I take this week based on this entry? _____

_____

_____

What would make this week great? _____

Notes: _____

_____

_____

WELCOME TO THE DARK SIDE

The world is full of light, and it is also full of darkness.

There is the sun and the moon,

Joy and pain,

Success and failure.

In life we see this too:

We feel great, then we get sick.

We take on a new client and lose a client.

We move forward then get knocked down.

But we need these moments to grow and appreciate all we have.

Many of us spend too much time avoiding the dark side, but we forget that the darkness is a privilege. Without, it we can't truly enjoy or appreciate the light.

This week, don't avoid or be afraid of the dark side. Accept it, because the light will follow.

Journal exercise date: _____/_____/_____

Quote: You can't be brave if only good things happen. (Mary Tyler Moore)

Takeaway from entry: _____

_____

_____

How does this entry relate to my life (personal or business)? _____

_____

_____

What action steps can I take this week based on this entry? _____

_____

_____

What would make this week great? _____

Notes: _____

_____

_____

THE BLACK DOT

One day, a professor entered his classroom and asked his students to prepare for a surprise test. They all waited anxiously at their desks for the exam to begin. The professor handed out the exams with the text facing down, as usual. Once he handed them all out, he asked the students to turn over the papers. To everyone's surprise, there were no questions–just a black dot in the center of the paper.

The professor, seeing the expression on everyone's faces, told them the following: "I want you to write about what you see there." The students, confused, got started on the inexplicable task.

At the end of the class, the professor took all the exams and started reading each one of them out loud in front of all the students.

All of them, with no exception, defined the black dot, trying to explain its position in the center of the sheet. After all had been read and the classroom was silent, the professor explained: "I'm not going to grade you on this, I just wanted to give you something to think about. No one wrote about the white part of the paper. Everyone focused on the black dot—and the same thing happens in our lives. We insist on focusing only on the black dot: the health issues that bother us, the lack of money, the complicated relationship with a family member, the disappointment with a client. The dark spots are very small when compared to everything we have in our lives, but they're the ones that pollute our minds."

This week, I challenge you to take your eyes away from the black dots in your life and instead focus on all that surrounds them. Enjoy each one of your blessings, each moment that life gives you. This week (and all other weeks), be happy and live a life filled with gratitude for all you have.

Journal exercise date: _____/_____/_____

Quote: Be happy for what you have while you work for what you want.
(Helen Keller)

Takeaway from entry: _____

_____

_____

How does this entry relate to my life (personal or business)? _____

_____

_____

What action steps can I take this week based on this entry? _____

_____

_____

What would make this week great? _____

Notes: _____

_____

_____

41

WELCOME HOME

An elderly carpenter was ready to retire. He told his employer-contractor of his plans to leave the house-building business to live a more leisurely life with his wife and to enjoy his extended family. He would miss the paycheck each week, but he wanted to retire. They could get by.

The contractor was sorry to see his good worker go and asked if he would build just one more house as a personal favor. The carpenter said yes, but over time it was easy to see that his heart wasn't in his work. He resorted to shoddy workmanship and used inferior materials. It was an unfortunate way to end a dedicated career.

When the carpenter finished his work, his employer came to inspect the house. Then he handed the front-door key to the carpenter and said, "This is your house—my gift to you."

The carpenter was shocked. And what a shame! If he only had known he was building his own house, he would have done it differently.

So it is with us. We build our lives a day at a time, often putting less than our best into the building. Then, with a shock, we realize we have to live in the house we've built. If we could do it over, we'd do it much differently.

But you can't go back. You are the carpenter, and every day you hammer a nail, place a board, or erect a wall. Someone once said, "Life is a do-it-yourself project." Your attitude and the choices you make today help build the "house" you will live in tomorrow.

This week, build wisely! You are constructing your house, so make sure it's one you wish to live in.

Journal exercise date: _____/_____/_____

Quote: You must have a solid foundation if you want a strong superstructure. (Gordon Hinkley)

Takeaway from entry: _____

_____

_____

How does this entry relate to my life (personal or business)? _____

_____

_____

What action steps can I take this week based on this entry? _____

_____

_____

What would make this week great? _____

Notes: _____

_____

_____

THE BUMBLE BEE

According to scientists, the bumblebee's body isn't built for flight; it's too heavy, and its wingspan is too small. Aerodynamically, the bumblebee cannot fly.

But the bumblebee doesn't know that. It doesn't know its limitations; it just knows it needs to fly in order to survive.

We put limits on ourselves every day. Limits tell us what we can or can't do or are capable of. But like the bumblebee, maybe we're better off not knowing. I wonder what we could do if we didn't know our limitations?

This week, push past your limits. Make your calls, talk with a stranger, try something new and exciting—and maybe a little scary. This week, go out and surprise yourself. You may just realize that you too can fly.

Journal exercise date: _____/_____/_____

Quote: Your wings already exist. All you have to do is fly.

Takeaway from entry: _____

_____

_____

How does this entry relate to my life (personal or business)? _____

_____

_____

What action steps can I take this week based on this entry? _____

_____

_____

What would make this week great? _____

Notes: _____

_____

_____

A STORM IS COMING

I heard an interesting story about buffalo and cows. Both animals live on plains. When a storm comes, the cows anticipate it and run east, hoping to outrun it. However, because they aren't superfast, inevitably they get caught right in the middle of the storm.

Unlike cows, buffalo turn west and run straight into the storm. By taking that approach, they get to the storm before it has time to form fully and therefore escape the nastiness of it.

How many times do we act like cows and try to outrun trouble? We may try to avoid it, hide from it, or even deny that a storm is coming, but when we do, we get caught in it anyway. And generally it's much worse than if we'd just faced it head-on.

This week, don't be afraid of the storm. You can handle it! Instead of running from it, turn and face it. You may find it isn't as bad as you thought it would be and that you can catch other storms before they get worse.

Journal exercise date: _____/_____/_____

Quote: After a storm comes calm. (Mathew Henry)

Takeaway from entry: _____

_____

_____

How does this entry relate to my life (personal or business)? _____

_____

_____

What action steps can I take this week based on this entry? _____

_____

_____

What would make this week great? _____

Notes: _____

_____

_____

WHAT IF?

Often we use the phrase "If only":

- If only I had more time.
- If only I had more money.
- If only I had more experience.

But what if you changed that statement to "what if?"

- What if I had more money? Then what would happen?
- What if I had more time? How would I use it?
- What if I had more experience? What would I know?

By asking "what if," you can focus on solutions and possibility. You can start to make changes. With "what if," you identify what you need, and you also know how it would change your world.

"If only" is a dream. "What if" is an action plan.

This week, act as if you already have what you need. You might be surprised and realize you have a lot more than you thought.

Journal exercise date: _____/_____/_____

Quote: Dwell in Possibility. (Emily Dickinson)

Takeaway from entry: _____

_____

_____

How does this entry relate to my life (personal or business)? _____

_____

_____

What action steps can I take this week based on this entry? _____

_____

_____

What would make this week great? _____

Notes: _____

_____

_____

CHANGE THE LENS

One of the things I enjoy is photography. I love looking at the world through a lens and exploring how it can be captured. I always find it amazing how one thing—a sunset, a tree, a person—can look so different based on the eye of the photographer and the lenses used.

When a photographer friend of mine doesn't like a particular setting or light source, he changes the lens. By changing the lens, the whole image changes; it becomes something completely new.

Sometimes I think we need to change the lens of our lives and the outlook we have. There are times when we don't particularly care for what we're doing, who we are with, or how things are turning out. But what if we changed the lens? What if, for just a moment, we shifted how we looked at it and how we approached it?

Every day we have the ability to refocus our thoughts—our lens of the world we live in—and open ourselves up to a new way of seeing things in front of us.

This week, what is something you're challenged with or not enjoying? How can you refocus that into something beautiful? Change your lens, and look for the new picture that comes from it.

Journal exercise date: _____/_____/_____

Quote: Your focus determines your reality. (George Lucas)

Takeaway from entry: _____

_____

_____

How does this entry relate to my life (personal or business)? _____

_____

_____

What action steps can I take this week based on this entry? _____

_____

_____

What would make this week great? _____

Notes: _____

_____

_____

MOVE THE BOULDER

In ancient times, a king had a boulder placed on a roadway. He hid himself from view and watched to see if anyone would remove the huge rock. Wealthy merchants and courtiers came by and simply walked around it. Many loudly blamed the king for not keeping the roads clear, but none did anything about getting the stone out of the way.

Then a peasant came along, carrying a load of vegetables. Upon approaching the boulder, the peasant laid down his burden and tried to move the stone to the side of the road. After much pushing and straining, he finally succeeded. When he picked up his load of vegetables, he noticed a purse lying in the road where the boulder had been. It contained many gold coins and a note from the king indicating that the gold was for the person who removed the boulder from the roadway.

The peasant learned what many of us never understand: every obstacle presents an opportunity to improve our condition.

So this is my question for you: what is lying in your path? Often we have obstacles that keep us from seeing the treasure that's right in front of us. The obstacle could be a task, a person, or perhaps a belief (which it often is). Regardless, we leave it and allow it to block us from the opportunity for greatness.

This week, move *your* boulder, and look for your treasure!

Journal exercise date: _____/_____/_____

Quote: The biggest obstacles are the barriers our own minds create.

Takeaway from entry: _____

_____

_____

How does this entry relate to my life (personal or business)? _____

_____

_____

What action steps can I take this week based on this entry? _____

_____

_____

What would make this week great? _____

Notes: _____

_____

_____

ALL OF ME

All life forms strive for the max of their potential, except human beings.

Think about that.

- How tall does a tree grow? As tall as it can.
- How fast does a cheetah run? As fast as it can.
- How high does a bird fly? As high as it can.

So, what makes humans different? Our ability to choose. We can choose what we do and also what we don't do.

- We make the choice to *be* part of ourselves or all of ourselves.
- We make the choice to enjoy all of life or part of life.
- We make the choice to develop all of ourselves or just part of ourselves.

How much of yourself are you giving—all or part?

This week, give all of you. Make the choice to be your best—and give your best. Live to your full potential. Don't leave anything behind. Use your choices to make your mark and be your best and fullest self.

Journal exercise date: _____/_____/_____

Quote: Don't worry about what it will take; just give it your all.

Takeaway from entry: _____

_____

_____

How does this entry relate to my life (personal or business)? _____

_____

_____

What action steps can I take this week based on this entry? _____

_____

_____

What would make this week great? _____

Notes: _____

_____

_____

LET ME TELL YOU
YOUR FUTURE

One of the more popular attractions at a carnival is the fortune teller. People love the mystique and the fun in having someone tell them the path of their future. Want me to tell your fortune today? I can.

You see, I too am a fortune teller. I can tell you exactly what your future will look like. All I need to do is look at your today. How you spend your day will give me all the information to know what your tomorrow will look like.

- Will you be successful? Let me look at your habits of success today.
- Will you have love and friendship? Let me look at how you make time for and treat your loved ones today?
- Will you have good health? Let me look at how you take care of yourself today.

Yes, I can tell your future—but so can you! If you want to ensure that your future holds the joys and life you want, stop waiting for a fortune teller to show you the way. Make your future *now*!

Journal exercise date: _____/_____/_____

Quote: Your choices today create your tomorrow.

Takeaway from entry: _____

_____

_____

How does this entry relate to my life (personal or business)? _____

_____

_____

What action steps can I take this week based on this entry? _____

_____

_____

What would make this week great? _____

Notes: _____

_____

_____

PLANT THE TREE

One of my favorite quotes comes from Confucius: "The best time to plant a tree was twenty years ago. The second-best time is today."

How many times do we focus on what we didn't accomplish yesterday, last week, or last year? The reality is, it doesn't matter. We no longer have yesterday; all we have is today. So if there was something you didn't get done, move forward and focus on doing it today (or at least take a step toward completing it today). Ask yourself, "What trees do you need to plant? And why?" If you get off track, think about the shade, the fruit, and the protection that tree can bring you in twenty years.

This week, don't focus on the seeds that weren't planted. Rather, focus on planting those seeds today. Twenty years from now, you'll be happy you did!

Journal exercise date: _____/_____/_____

Quote: If you're waiting for a sign, this is it!

Takeaway from entry: _____

_____

_____

How does this entry relate to my life (personal or business)? _____

_____

_____

What action steps can I take this week based on this entry? _____

_____

_____

What would make this week great? _____

Notes: _____

_____

_____

50

THE ORANGE

When Dr. Wayne Dyer was preparing to speak at an I Can Do It conference, he decided to bring an orange on stage with him as a prop for my lecture. He opened a conversation with a bright young fellow of about twelve, who was sitting in the front row.

"If I were to squeeze this orange as hard as I could, what would come out?" I asked him.

He looked at me like I was a little crazy and said, "Juice, of course."

"Do you think apple juice could come out of it?"

"No!" he laughed.

"What about grapefruit juice?"

"No!"

"What would come out of it?"

"Orange juice, of course."

"Why? Why when you squeeze an orange does orange juice come out?"

He may have been getting a little exasperated with me at this point. "Well, it's an orange and that's what's inside."

He continued, "Let's assume that this orange isn't an orange, but it's you. And someone squeezes you, puts pressure on you, says something you don't like, offends you. And out of you comes anger, hatred, bitterness, fear. Why? The answer, as our young friend has told us, is because that's what's inside."

This is one of the great lessons of life. What comes out when life squeezes you? When someone hurts or offends you? If anger, pain, and fear come out of you, it's because that's what's inside. It doesn't matter who does the squeezing—your mother, your brother, your children, your boss, the government. If someone says something about you that you don't like, whatever comes out of you is what's inside. And what's inside is up to you; it's your choice.

This week, when life puts pressure on you, come from a better place—a place of kindness, generosity, and grace. You have greatness in you, so let that be what comes out when you get a little squeeze.

Journal exercise date: _____/_____/_____

Quote: Happiness isn't determined by what's around you, but rather what's inside you.

Takeaway from entry: _____

_____

_____

How does this entry relate to my life (personal or business)? _____

_____

_____

What action steps can I take this week based on this entry? _____

_____

_____

What would make this week great? _____

Notes: _____

_____

_____

STANDING STILL

Do you remember the Scarecrow in *The Wizard of Oz*? As he sat attached to his post, he explained some choices to Dorothy, saying, "Well, you can go this way, or you can go that way. This way is good, but then so is that way." His indecision was frustrating.

Indecision can do this to us; it can confuse and also paralysis. On the surface, indecision might seem safe, but really it's one of the biggest curses on our growth and ability to live a fulfilled life. Having the ability to decide and choose a direction frees us and opens us up to opportunity and life.

Often we get stuck in indecision because we fear making the wrong choice and going in the wrong direction. But here's the thing: if you start down the wrong path, you'll figure it out. So there's no need to fear! It may take time and may put you a little behind, but you will figure it out and get back on the right road.

So this week, pick a road to travel. Decide and move forward. Remember, you can go this way, or you can go that way. But standing still gets you nowhere.

Journal exercise date: _____/_____/_____

Quote: In the middle of difficulty lies opportunity. (Albert Einstein)

Takeaway from entry: _____

_____

_____

How does this entry relate to my life (personal or business)? _____

_____

_____

What action steps can I take this week based on this entry? _____

_____

_____

What would make this week great? _____

Notes: _____

_____

_____

GROW

When a seed is planted, it needs a few things to grow: fertile soil, water, nutrients, and sun. Without these, a seed isn't able to sustain life and grow into its beauty.

Like the seed, we also need a few key ingredients to become our best. Ask yourself:

- Am I planted in the correct soil? Do I have the right surroundings in my office and with the people I'm spending time with?
- Am I getting the right nutrients? Do I feed my mind daily with positive thoughts of success?
- Am I allowing sun in? Or am I shading myself from my own light?

This week, check and make sure you're planted correctly, and allow yourself the opportunity to grow into your greatness.

Journal exercise date: _____/_____/_____

Quote: Deep in their roots, flowers meet the light. (Theodore Roosevelt)

Takeaway from entry: _____

_____

_____

How does this entry relate to my life (personal or business)? _____

_____

_____

What action steps can I take this week based on this entry? _____

_____

_____

What would make this week great? _____

Notes: _____

_____

_____

CLOSING THOUGHTS OF CLARA-TY

Thank you for taking this fifty-two-week journey to gain insight and clarity for a happy and fulfilled life. Keep this journal close, and reflect on the words and thoughts you came away with. Remember this:

- It isn't about being perfect; just be perfectly you.
- Keep moving forward.
- Forgive yourself and others.
- Allow for happiness and gratitude daily.
- Start each day with an open heart, a passion for living fully, and acceptance of who you are.

All the best you for today, tomorrow, and forward.

Clara

Clara Capano is a sought after trainer, speaker and coach. If you would like to hire Clara for one of your events or for personal coaching, please reach her at (303) 956-2309 or www.clara-ty.com.

Printed in the United States
By Bookmasters